LIFE CYCLES
Salamanders

by Robin Nelson

first step nonfiction

Lerner Publications Company · Minneapolis

Look at the salamander.

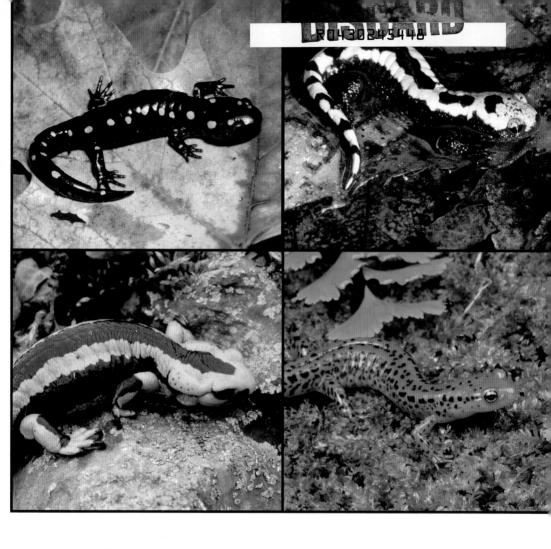

There are many kinds of salamanders.

Like a frog, a salamander is an **amphibian**.

How does a salamander grow?

A salamander starts as an egg.

Salamander eggs **float** in water.

A **larva** grows in the egg.

The larva **hatches**.

At first, the larva looks like
a fish.

It swims and breathes like a fish too.

Later, the larva grows legs.

The larva eats.

The larva keeps growing
bigger.

It becomes a salamander.

This salamander is grown up.

It is fun to watch a
salamander grow.

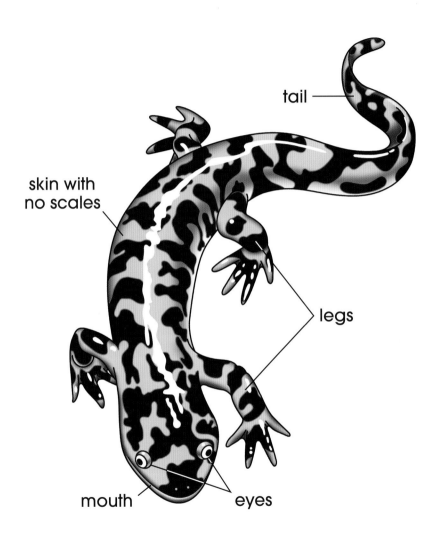

tail

skin with
no scales

legs

mouth

eyes

Adult Salamanders

Adult salamanders have many body parts. Salamanders have four legs. They have a long tail. Their tail will break off if it is grabbed. Then the salamander will grow a new tail.

When the weather turns cold, most salamanders hibernate, or sleep. When they wake up, they eat insects, worms, snails, and small fish. In the spring, female salamanders lay their eggs, and a new salamander life cycle begins.

Salamander Facts

 Salamanders are cold-blooded. This means when the air or water is cold, their bodies become cold.

 There are three kinds of salamanders. One kind lives its whole life in the water. Another kind lives its whole life on land. The third kind lives both on land and in the water.

 Salamanders drink and breathe through their skin.

Salamanders don't make any sounds because they can't hear sounds.

Adult salamanders are about 4 to 8 inches long.

As salamanders grow, they lose their outer layer of old skin and eat it.

The largest kind of salamander can grow to be over 5 feet long. This kind lives in Japan.

Glossary

 amphibian – an animal with slimy skin that lives its life in water and on land

 float – to be held up in water

 hatches – comes out of an egg

 larva – a baby salamander that lives in the water

Index

The images in this book are used with the permission of: © John Parke/Visuals Unlimited, p. 2; © Dwight R. Kuhn, pp. 3 (top left), 6, 8, 9, 12, 22 (second from bottom); © age fotostock/ SuperStock, pp. 3 (top right, bottom left); © George Grall/National Geographic/Getty Images, p. 3 (bottom right); © Sergey Rogovets/Dreamstime.com, pp. 4, 22 (top); © Lynn Stone/Animals Animals, p. 5; © Todd Pusser/naturepl.com, pp. 7, 22 (second from top); © E.R. Degginger/ Animals Animals, p. 10; © Altrendo Nature/Getty Images, pp. 11, 22 (bottom); © Allen Blake Sheldon/Animals Animals, p. 13; © Tom McHugh/Photo Researchers, Inc., p. 14; © Gerold and Cynthia Merker/Visuals Unlimited/Getty Images, p. 15; © Gilbert Twiest/Visuals Unlimited, p. 16; © David M. Dennis/Animals Animals, p. 17; © Laura Westlund/Independent Picture Service, p. 18.
Front Cover: © Parke H. John, Jr./Visuals Unlimited/Getty Images.

Lerner Publications Company
A division of Lerner Publishing Group, Inc.
241 First Avenue North
Minneapolis, MN 55401 U.S.A.

Website address: www.lernerbooks.com

Library of Congress Cataloging-in-Publication Data

Nelson, Robin, 1971–
    Salamanders / by Robin Nelson.
        p.   cm. — (First step nonfiction. Animal life cycles)
    Includes index.
    ISBN 978–0–7613–4065–2 (lib. bdg. : alk. paper)
    1. Salamanders—Juvenile literature. I. Title.
QL668.C2N45 2009
597.8'5—dc22   2008025712

Manufactured in the United States of America
1 2 3 4 5 6 – DP – 14 13 12 11 10 09